Dear Reader,

    Whether you knew me from social media or just happened to stumble upon this while trying to search up a book about the actual planet Pluto, I'm still happy that you ended up here.

    I always believed that the things that belong to you always come back, and maybe that's why I decided to write this book. Some of these entries are dedicated to specific people and some aren't, but nevertheless they all mean something to me and I hope they mean something to you.

    I hope you don't make the same mistakes I've made. Tell people you care about them when they are still around. Appreciate people when they are still around. Don't take anyone for granted. Don't look at people as temporary, because they *aren't*. If they belong to you, you will always meet them again. Maybe in this life or the next.

    So, even though I'm pretty late, these are all the things I wanted to say but never got the chance to. Once again, I'm sorry all of this is a little bit to late.

                Till next time,

                      Pluto

Until We Meet Again

pluto

for the ones who will come back

(and for the ones who won't)

Until We Meet Again

© 2016 Ileena 'Pluto' Irving. All rights reserved.

Published by Lulu

Originally Published in the United States by Lulu Press in 2016.

No part of this work may be reproduced without written permission from the publisher, except brief quotations for review purposes.

This is a work of fiction. Any resemblance to real characters, places or events is purely coincidental.

Cover design by:

M1SAKA
http://m1saka.tumblr.com

ISBN 978-1-365-29384-9

THE BEGINNING OF THE END

there will be a day when I will leave you.

don't take it personally, if you knew me as well as you thought you did this wouldn't be such a surprise. odds are that I already left you and now you're scrambling for answers. pillaging my notebooks and laptop hoping that the answer is hidden between the lines of coffee stained pages and dogeared books.

i guess this is the answer you're looking for.

I'm sorry to say this but this won't be much of an answer that you'd enjoy. If you want a blatant answer to why I left you and why I'm never coming back, you won't be able to find it. It's not something you find — the answer is not a lost idea wanting to be found, it's just not for your knowledge. If you think really hard, a lot of things aren't for your knowledge.

That's besides the point though.

Before I disappear I want to tell you a few things I couldn't tell you in person. Probably because I was too scared, or afraid that I'll say something I don't mean. Either way, I never got to mention it before I left.

This is what this is for I guess.

AIM

I feel like I should apologize but in all honesty I won't mean it. I always knew I was going to leave and I always hinted to you that I would and you always didn't believe me or just never even noticed.

My intention was never to tell you anyway. You were cooped up in your whole life that mine was just an addition to yours. Even when you wanted to ask things about me, and I would shockingly open up to you, you didn't care. and it's not like you could've done something to change my past so why would you always ask about it anyway.

You will never know me, no matter how many times you call me your soulmate. That only pushes me further away. I am no ones soulmate, not anymore.

It's like you wanted me to hurt you, you wanted me to rip you to shreds.

I don't love you anymore.
But I used to.
At least know that.

WAIT

when we were together and in a good mood, we were fucking electric. we could light the sky on fire if we wanted to.

but that's the thing

we played with fire and we ended up burning everything we built.

I remember the bad things you've said and done to people and I remember changing myself and the way I acted just to keep you happy.
You're toxic — *we were toxic.*
People were physically and emotionally scared of us. The way you spoke to people made them feel inhuman
how could you live with that?

So I told you about all the things I hated about you.
that was one of my high accomplishments. I was always afraid of telling people what I really wanted to say and you were the only person I did that to.

Sure, it backfired and you took everyone I cared about with you and I was left alone again — but it felt good at least.

We won't ever talk again, I'm sure of it. But I still
hope you get what you deserve
this sounds like I wish misfortune upon you and honestly I don't even know if I do

FIRE

I wish I met a lot of people sooner. Maybe they would've changed me for the better or teach me things I learned later in life. I say this because there are some people I should've met earlier.
And then there's you.
Who I thought I should've met earlier but realized that was a bloody mistake and it was a good thing I met you later in life so the pain you brought upon me would not hurt as much as it would've.

yea that sounds more like it.

I swear that if you saw my bare back you would be shocked with all the engraved scars. You'd probably wonder how many people I have hurt that caused them to impale a knife into my back.

The answer is a lot.
and each scar, whether minuscule or titanic, has a name right next to them. a story laced between the new flesh and traces of the old.
stories you'd rather not hear
not because they are bad but because you don't give a shit about me.
you're just curious, you don't care
in the end it is I that has to fix whatever I broke
telling you about my trials and tribulations are a waste of your time and mine

but you know what

one day someone is going to ask and one day I'm going to tell them
I'm going to let all my demons spill onto the floor and I'm not going to care who has the courage to clean them up.

one day someone is going to listen
not just hear, *listen*
and they are not going to look at me like a burning building
they are going to look at me like I am a skyscraper
and i'm going to be so high and so bright the sun will be reflecting off of me

and you're going to be too small and too dull for my eyes to see

I REALLY HOPE YOU LOVED ME TOO

this is going to be messy and I think you know it will be too. so I'll try to make this as easy as I can, but I can't promise anything.

so lets drown this shot and hope for the better.

HEADSTART

I noticed you first. I liked you first. I wanted to hear your voice first. I wanted to hold you first. I wanted to see you laugh first. I wanted, more than anything, to be your first.

How it happened is messy, weird, awkward, amazing, unforgettable, problematic....

but you were my first too.

you can take this *first* as PG or NC-17 as you want
but it won't matter in the end

I want to write about you in metaphors and analogies
I want to compare you to a breath of fresh air or a band around my chest
I want to say you were mine
but we both know you weren't

in the simplest of ways:
we were two teenagers wanting to have a bit of fun before our time was up and the adult world would have us by our necks

and that was us
and that's all

CLIMAX

I wanted to tell you about myself.
this sounds so trivial but let me explain.

I wanted to tell you about *myself*
I wanted to step out of my clothes and stand there
completely vulnerable in front of you
and I wanted you to still look into my eyes
and I wanted you to ask me about my past
and my family
and my fears
and everything you never dared to ask before

but most importantly
I wanted you to listen
I wanted you to *know*

but instead you looked at my body when I was vulnerable
and you saw me as desire
and you looked at me in lust
and you didn't ask about my past
or my family
or my fears
or anything

you didn't say anything

RESOLVING ACTION

I ended up being the one to decide our future.
I don't know how the hell that happened but the job just
landed onto my lap and I was too late in noticing it.

So, in the most simplest of terms, I ended us.
Not that we even started anyway.
(not that it felt that way)

You don't really talk about your feelings
and neither do I — so we were just fucked by then

I wanted more
I *deserved* more
and frankly
you deserved better

so I'm leaving
and odds are you'll never see me again
((and I'm not just saying that because seriously
you'll never see me again))

and the worst part is that
I can't even be mad at you for that

this one is on me

GRAND FINALE

so here it is. the big confession time. the huge crescendo. the conclusion of this regurgitation of words.

~~I love you~~.
Correction.
I loved you.

and you know what?
it was amazing. I'm very happy you were the person I chose to love first. I'm happy I saw you one day and thought —

Him. I want him.

and I'm happy I actually fucking had you. I'm so happy we were both each others first in multiple aspects. We were so scared, but we both didn't mind taking the risk. We were both so unsure of ourselves, but one look at you and I was home. We were messy, and awkward, and bewildered, and dangerous and I was so much in fucking love with you I confused it with being mad at you all the time.

Yea, we could've been better.
That goes without saying.
Maybe if we communicated more and actually talked about our feelings. Maybe if we tried harder and weren't afraid of the consequences. Maybe if you loved me.

Yea, maybe if you loved me too this would've all worked out.

but nevertheless
I'm happy it was you.

I'm happy I chose you.

and that's the end of us
but god damn it was a pretty good run wasn't it?

DON'T SAY IT UNTIL YOU MEAN IT

the first time you said *I love you* was on Valentines day.
On the way back to my house, on a winding street lined with pine trees
You said it as a joke, and that's why I laughed

the second time you said *I love you* was when we were on your living room floor
vinyls upon vinyls with the wrapping all around us
this time I just ignored it and gave a tight smile

the third time you said *I love you* it was attached to a quick goodbye on the phone
I hung up before I could react and dropped to the floor right after

because how the fuck could you ever love me and not know about the planet of skeletons I have in my closest?
you never seen my bad days or my worst days
you don't know about the way I light up and the way I fade away
you don't know about the voices in my head or the numbers on my arm dialing a phone home
hell, you don't even know what that means

you can't love me because you don't even know that I'm a planet
you can't love me because you don't know that I gave up being a human a long time ago
and you can **never** love me because you'll never understand why

THE 3 AM LONGING

Come to me

with those light eyes illuminating in the darkness
filled with *lust, hope, dust… maybe even love*

Walk slowly

with each step
making small vibrations in the house I wish to call my home
I want to hear every creak and every whine it makes
I want to hear it breathe

Don't rush
Take your time

I want to see your chest rise and fall — quickening with each step you take towards me
I want you to bite your bottom lip, or run your tongue over it
I want to see your eyes look me over.

You don't look at me like you only want me in your bed
but with you, completely.
like you want to see me in your next life
(and the one after that)
like I was the Garden of Eden and you were Adam
like I just became your favorite song or movie
like I was a dream; the one you'll never forget

Hold your hand out now

let me see the blood pulse through your veins
let the anticipation build up

Be steady as you come closer
I can smell you now,
hints of your cologne from this morning
and a rush of your soap from the shower just now

I hear you say my name from your lips
barely a whisper
barely even heard
but my skin pricks nevertheless

I'm yearning for you
Come to me
Come to me and never go back to where you were before
Come to me
Come to me

come to me

IF YOU'RE WONDERING ABOUT WHERE I'LL BE

in the last lines of books
in the tip of your broken pencil
in the crevice of your bookshelf
(yes the one with all the dust)

in the shadows of your room
in the shadows of your town
in the shadows
period

in the bullet of a gun
in the wound
in the heart on your sleeve
in the dirt underneath your fingernails

in that box you called OLD THINGS
in the drawer where your sharp things are
in the letter you'll never open
in the phone call you'll never pick up

in the home you don't call a home
in the next life you won't be ready for
in the smile of your lover
in the screams of your enemy

in the flash of a black car speeding down the highway
in the plane you missed

in this book
in this sentence

WHOLE

I have never been incomplete

Yes, it has felt that I have had holes in my chest
and burns on my hands
and bones sticking out of my ribcage

there are some days when I just want a body to hold
and someone to say cliche sentences like *it'll get better*

there are some days when I can't get out of bed
and I can't eat
or drink
or sleep
and I'm just staring at the wall with no thoughts in my mind

there are some days when God doesn't seem real
and the skies don't look blue anymore
and my skin feels hard
and my teeth ache from clenching them shut

Yes, it has felt that I am broken in all the right places
but **never once** have I ever been incomplete

"ARE YOU ANGRY?"

I want to light the sky on fire
I want to see the clouds burn

I want to obliterate universes and crush them in the palm of
my hand
or take stars and throw them down peoples throats

I want to plant trees in people and watch nature take back
what belongs to them
I want to toss comets in your closet and watch all the
secrets you've been hiding turn into stardust

I want to cause pain in the most aesthetic of ways
and I want it to fucking hurt

now say it for the people in the back

I WILL NEVER LOOK AT YOU LIKE A BURNING HOME
YOU ARE NOT BROKEN
JUST HURT IN MANY WAYS

I WON'T TRY TO FIX YOU UNLESS YOU **ASK ME TO**

I WILL NEVER LET YOU GO TO SLEEP UNSETTLED
WE ARE GOING TO STAY UP, NOT LOOK AT THE CLOCK ONCE, AND TALK IT OUT
WHATEVER IT MIGHT BE

I WILL NEVER BE AFRIAD OF YOU
YOU ARE NOT A MONSTER
YOU JUST HAVE A LOT OF EMOTIONS AND BAGGAGE AND STRESS
AND SOMETIMES IT'S HARD TO HOLD ALL THREE AT ONCE

I WON'T TRY TO HOLD ANYTHING UNLESS YOU **ASK ME TO**

I WILL LISTEN TO YOU
I WILL SIT AND LET YOU YELL AND SCREAM AND BREAK THINGS TO GET ALL OF THE DARKNESS OUT OF YOUR BLOODSTREAM
I WILL HOLD YOU WHEN YOU ARE DONE
AND REMIND YOU OF HOW I WILL ALWAYS BE HERE

WHETHER WE END UP TOGETHER OR NOT

I WILL ALWAYS BE HERE
I WILL ALWAYS BE HERE

AND I WON'T STOP SAYING THAT UNTIL YOU
BELIEVE IT

BECAUSE: I LOVE YOU EDITION

I love you because you take me in all my shapes and forms. You understand that I'm malleable, but you'd still want me as the way I'm supposed to be

I love you because you make me laugh so hard that tears fall from my eyes. And you know I hate crying in public, and only by laughing will I show my vulnerability

I love you because you're just as a weird lame nerd as I am

I love you because I can say anything I want, no matter how disgusting. You still think my blood is pure, and I feel clean

I love you because you want to get to know me. It terrifies me, but you're all in

I love you because you're all in

I love you because you make me feel like I'm not entirely alone

I love you because you still listen to me when I'm completely wrong

I love you because you tell me when I'm being an insensitive prick, even when I hate it

I love you because you have the potential of staying with me

I love you because it feels like you're the one that's not temporary

I HAVE NO PATIENCE

I waited for you.

I gave you time when there was no more to give.
I let you start fires and say words you didn't mean.
I allowed you to leave because I ~~knew~~ thought you would come back

I waited for you to come back

but leaving as easy as you came was your specialty
it seemed like a weight was lifted off your shoulders when you walked away

was I really that much of a burden?
did I break your chest?
did I fracture one of your ribs?

well I fucking hope I did
I hope I broke something
and I hope it **never** heals

I'M BLAMING YOU

i don't think anyone looked at me the way you did

i think that's what fucked me up

CONFESSIONS

I'm trying to be better
but for who?

7/25/15

One of these days I'm going to get on a train
or bus
or plane
or car
and leave, with no intention of coming back

I'll save up a lot, get all my clothes and information, and
just drive until I feel home

I always knew I would leave everything behind, but even
though I feel guilty, I regret nothing

I've been trapped my whole life
I just endured and assimilated
Now, I just want to belong somewhere.

I don't know where that place is
but I know it's beautiful

SILVER SCREEN BLUES

you know maybe this is how it ends
with a good melancholy song and a nice camera shot of you
walking away from me —
or vice versa

we can turn back around just once and look at each other
remembering the memories and the fights and the love
remembering all the love we had for each other

and then we'd nod
(like every fucking cliche movie)
as if we both were in understanding of life and we finally
get what God is doing and our purpose for living isn't so
confusing anymore

and then we'd give a light smile
as if we were saying —
it's over, but I'm damn happy it happened
and we'd continue to walk away
allowing the sad music and credits to follow

yea maybe that's how this should end

I'M NOT GETTING BETTER

I'm sorry for all the pain I caused you
I took you for granted and didn't appreciate you
and now our time is up and I'm looking back realizing that
I royally fucked up everything

I said things I shouldn't have said to the wrong people
I did things I shouldn't have done to the wrong people
I trusted people I shouldn't have
I made the same damn mistakes over and over and over
again

I'm surprised you don't hate me
after all the bruises and tears I gave you
after pushing you to the side and finding other people
then realizing that the other people were fucks and I came
running back to you knowing you'd take me back

I'm really fucking surprised you don't hate my guts
honestly if you wanted to give me a black eye or something
of the sort I'd let you do it

THE CLOUD BOY

There was once a boy who loved playing in the clouds
He could imagine them to be anything and anyone
so he was never lonely

One day, while playing in the clouds
he caught sight of a girl

Her hair was tied up in two ponytails and her long bangs
made a shield for her eyes
Her shirt reached up to her neck and was the color of love
Her skirt hem dragged rocks being her and her small toes
were covered by shiny black boots
and she walked with the sun trailing behind her

and the cloud boy was utterly fascinated by her

But the boy couldn't talk to her; every time he tried she
would not listen
So the boy floated by her every day
wanting nothing more than to be at her side

He stayed to hear her hearty laughter and see her smile
even if she was missing her two front teeth

The boy stayed by her side when her father would come
home late, stumbling around the house
and when her mother would cry while ripping white
envelopes

The boy stayed by her side when the other kids at school
would make fun of her for her worn out clothes

But now its been years since the boy first saw the girl
He watched as her two ponytails turned to one then to none
and the boy watched as her shirt lowered down to her chest,
and turned into the color of despair

He watched as her skirt grew shorter and how her small
toes were now exposed in tall high heels

the cloud boy's heart ached for her
but no matter how hard he tried he couldn't help her
she wouldn't listen

and yet the boy still floated by her everyday
wanting nothing more than to hold her hand

the boy watched as her laughter changed into coughs
and how her smile suddenly disappeared

He watched as she started to hide her arms more
and stopped looking at both sides of the road before
crossing

Now it has been a few months
since the cloud boy left the girl

and the only reason he left was because, after all these
years, he still couldn't find out the color of her eyes

THE PERFECT CUP OF TEA

I always walk up the stairs with a cup of tea filled to the brim. Not even walking, just taking small steps periodically just in case the tea spilled.

Sometimes I made it to the top and sometimes I spilled it and I would have to go back downstairs, go to the kitchen, get a paper towel, wipe up the mess, throw the towel away, and try again.

It was a very tedious task.

My mother used to yell at me for the times I get too lazy to clean up the mess and just allow the tea to dry up on the floor to stick

when I was twelve I realized how many times I allowed the tea to dry up on the floor. most of the time I didn't even care if all the tea spill by the time I got to the last staircase. the boiling hot tea spilling on my feet and the carpet and the granite didn't bother me like it should've.

maybe i liked how the tea burned my feet
maybe I was too busy to notice the abundance of spills
maybe I just didn't care

finally my mother, being as explosive as she is, broke all the teacups and threw away all the tea we had in the house

in all honestly I freaked out

I could've ripped the whole house from its foundation and
throw it towards the horizon. I could've taken matches and
burn the place down letting it's ashes fill the toxic sky
I could've done all that

but I didn't

I just disintegrated into my covers
and let my bed seep me in
like tea leaves
brewing

and like the perfect cup of tea I finally became that dark
rich color with the perfect amount of milk and sugar
placed into a saucer that was the perfect size; in which the
ridges kept me in place and the walk upstairs wasn't so bad
anymore

REACH FOR THE SKY

don't hit the moon on the way up kid

TO THE GIRL I USED TO BE

1. I'm sorry you were ashamed of your body. It wasn't your fault you had C cups in 6th grade while every other girl had A's. I mean you got C's on every math test while everyone else got A's so there's not really a difference. But you didn't have to wear that big bulky jacket every single day. You could've at least washed it. not only did you wear that jacket to school, you wore it home. you wore it with your parents. you wore in the shower. you wore it even when you took it off. you wore it under the covers of your sheets. you didn't dare look at yourself, and I'm sorry you didn't learn how to love yourself sooner. you didn't have to wear two bras everyday to make sure everything was held down. you didn't have to give up being a ballet dancer. you could've done all of that with a big chest. people have done more. I can't believe that you were actually mad at your mother for her genetics. you were actually mad at your fucking anatomy and the inevitable. how dumb can you be? who cares if you have big boobs or not! if you want to wear that fucking tight shirt, by God wear it. wear the shit out of it. because even though most people forget that your eyes are on your face, you can always make them remember. and never forget.

2. I'm sorry for not loving you enough. I should have treated you better. I should have treated your body better. I'm sorry for all the scars and hunger pains. I'm sorry for all the screams no one heard. why did you listen to them when they said shut up? you should have kept your mouth open, letting your opinions slip through your teeth even if you got in trouble.

you were so confused. you thought too much and compared yourself to everyone with a heartbeat. I'm sorry you hated the skin you lived in. you shouldn't have listen to them. you shouldn't have listened to that 7 page letter about how worthless and ugly you were and how if mr. green eyes and you were in a room together he would rather die or turn gay before falling in love with you. you shouldn't have forgiven the person who wrote it. you shouldn't have stayed friends with her. God, you were so narrow minded. I wish you loved yourself. I wish you thought that without a contradicting thought. And if loving yourself makes you a selfish bitch then you are one beautiful selfish bitch.

3. I didn't mean to hate everything in the world. I didn't mean to hate human kind and waking up in the morning. I'm sorry for wanting to forget everything. I'm sorry for wanting to start over. I'm sorry for surrounding you with people who put you down and made you feel ugly and dumb and fucking worthless. I'm sorry for making you have to go through hell over and over and over again. I'm sorry for giving you a reason to wear long sleeves. I'm sorry that I realized all of this a little bit too late.

4. I'm not sorry for changing my name. I'm not sorry for finally finding out who the fuck I am. I will never say that name that I used to be called because that girl was dumb and allowed people to influence her so much that she didn't even think her own thoughts. I'm not sorry for pushing people away who didn't deserve my presence. I'm not sorry for leaving.

because I realized how beautiful the world is and how amazing and stupid and mean and totally fascinating everything and everyone is. and not everyone is as horrendous as you think cause you will find someone with such a damn beautiful mind that you won't even be able to fathom it.

5. I'm not here to remind you of all the fucking shit you've done to yourself and to everyone around you. I'm here to tell you, that you're going to be okay. cause you're going to find people who have the same heartbeat as you do. you'll be okay. you'll be okay. *you'll be okay*

NOT SORRY

they say once you date a writer you'll never die

so you're welcome

i made you fucking immortal

NO N. SENSE

Dear —,

    I don't know whether to apologize for whom I've become or whom I haven't become. Both are kind of overlapping and it makes me confused at times. Should I apologize for being confusing as well? (I think I should).

    I think I spend too much time looking at my bedroom ceiling. I'm waiting for the top to blow off and for me to fall upwards into something. It sounds mad but it makes sense to me. I'm being confusing again, aren't I?

    I also spend too much time looking out my window, looking for something that I wish was there but never will be. I realize that I look at many things like that. I look at my family that way, my teachers that way, my grades that way, the person I love that way, even myself that way. I've convinced myself that looking will possibly (in some unknown and impossible way) make what's not there simply appear.

    Damn, I am being confusing again.

    I'm scared of change you know. At least a part of me is. It's like I'm stuck in this constant state of fear and comfortableness. It just makes me go insane sometimes. I guess that's what makes me human. But I don't particularly want to be human anymore. Not now at least, not with everything thats going on. I feel like if some alien species can look into our planet right now and see all the shit we fucked up they would thank whoever their God is that they aren't human.

    I'm at that point right now, if you're wondering. My dissociation is kicking in a bit, have you realized? I look at things (shocker!) and well I can't really describe it. It's there and it's not there and it means nothing and everything and maybe something more all at the same time. It's bloody mad I tell you, it hurts my head sometimes.

I apologize once again for another letter full of nonsense. I don't really know why you want me to write all of these letters. They don't really help whatever I'm feeling, it just makes me put them into words. And not good ones at that.

I'm shaking right now. My right hand is shaking again, so maybe I'm afraid of something. I hate when my hand does that because sometimes I can tell what's making me fearful, but most times (like this one) I can't. It's like some outside force I can't put my finger on that makes me nervous about everything.

Well, I hope everything on your side is better than mine. I'll write to you again soon. And I promise next time it will make sense.

                              apologetically,
                                        ___

FOR THE NIGHTS I CAN'T REMEMBER

I'm lying when I told you I didn't remember what we said.
I blamed it on the substances of the empty bottles around
my feet
I didn't want to ruin the time we spent together
I didn't want to ruin the stomach hurting laughter
and the trips and falls and complete slur of words

but I do remember what we said

I remember saying that you'll find better people and forget
all about me. I remember you agreeing. but I also
remember you looking into my eyes and saying that you
couldn't forget me. and then you'd hold me closer, kiss me
some more, and try to make me forget

I remember holding onto you for dear life because I was
afraid you'd slip through my fingertips. I remember feeling
like I could never get enough of you. I remember feeling
intoxicated and it wasn't from the alcohol. I remember
hating myself for letting you get under my skin and into my
bloodstream.

I remember that I wanted to forget.

but even alcohol couldn't make me forget the way I felt
about you

(maybe this is one of the reasons why underage drinking is
illegal)

VOICE MEMO 7/23/16

even with all the things I have and am blessed with and are grateful for I still feel unsatisfied I still feel that I want more. and hearing that you're probably thinking *wow this girl is really selfish and narcissistic and materialistic* but I don't just mean things. cause of course I want more things everyone does. I am a human being, I will always want things. But I'm talking about something more. not physical. emotionally, I want something more. I want people to care more. I want people to reciprocate more.

I can't really explain it but I know that I feel unsatisfied. I feel like when I have a conversation with someone I feel unsatisfied with what I hear. I feel unsatisfied with a lot of people's responses lately. I don't really know if that's a me problem or people just aren't giving me what I want. and it does sound selfish and maybe it is selfish but I deserve more. I deserve something that I don't have to touch but I can feel. There's a lot of people in my life and only a couple make me feel something.

I think the most disappointing thing is wanting that one person you really want to have that one connection with and there's just nothing because you still feel unsatisfied with what they say and you analyze them completely and that's just it. It's not that they don't have any depth, but what you see is what you get. and that's fine, but I personally want more. this probably makes me seem like a bad person, but I can't stop feeling this need and want to feel more. and I feel like there's so much I'm not feeling or seeing or experiencing and it fucking ruins me.

THERE HAS TO BE SOMEONE

I am who I am for the good of humanity
and if that means being the monster under your bed
the villain in a fairy tail
the victimizer
the murderer
the ghost of your deepest nightmare
or the devil himself

then so be it

WHEN THE SUN RISES

8:45 PM - Saturday Evening:

The lights are way too bright for my liking. I personally prefer a dark shadow than seeing an HD man wearing a blue blazer trying to get my number. His hands are fiddling with his drink and his eyes keep darting to my chest just to check if I do have them. You know, just in case they were going to disappear. A headache is already coming on while my friend is having the time of her life. I want to have the time of my life too, but instead I'm stuck playing designated driver and talking to a man way too old and way too drunk. I keep checking my phone, hoping for time to move on quicker or just for ~~someone~~ anyone to get my attention. Someone worth my attention. Then, of course with my line of pessimistic thoughts, I begin to wish I wasn't so fucking sad all the time. Then I start to think:

maybe I shouldn't be here. maybe we all shouldn't be here; getting so intoxicated that we can't speak, or trying to blow out our ears with this horrendous music, or attempt to talk to people who obviously aren't here to sit down and get to know you.

I start thinking that this was all a mistake, and I start to believe it. All the while this poor excuse for a man has passed out and I'm stuck with his stench and slurred slumber. I look over to my friend and an ache enters my chest and I wonder how long the black hole has been there. I wonder if my heart was the first to go.

Then I turn to go.

9:00 PM

I'm standing next to a girl heaving her guts out while I wait outside the booming room with alcohol bursting from its seams. I wonder how it got to this. I wonder if it has even changed. The partying, the stench, the designated driver, the yearning to feel something other than the black hole in my chest causing me to disappear from the inside out.

I always wanted more but I never really knew what more was. I don't feel alone and I surround myself with people and they don't hate my existence but they don't particularly care about it either.

I find myself walking away from the loud music and I don't really know where I'm headed. I may even be lost already, but it's the most quiet its ever been and I take a deep breath without the smell of drugs or the stench of alcohol and sweat.

And its the sweetest breath of air I've ever taken.

9:18 PM

A train station. I ended up at a train station. I start wondering what the hell is wrong with me while I wrap my fleece around my body and buy a ticket.

Now I know I'm insane. But I keep on going. I keep on walking. I don't even know where the ticket leads me, but I keep on moving.

The train station at 9:18 PM has to be the sketchiest place but I still feel a sense of safety in the unknown. So me and my insanity board the train and I pick a seat near the window. Because I want to see what I'm leaving behind.

I want to see it zoom past me and feel a weight leave my body every single mile.

My body is buzzing with a sense of excitement and I realize that I'm not shaking because I'm scared but because this feels like the only right thing I've done in my life.

I see the train start to move now and everything I've known pass by and I've never felt so free in my life. I feel the *more* I wanted come closer to me than it ever has before.

I want something new. I want *someone* new. I need to talk to someone and I want them to understand. I want to cry and not feel guilty about it. I want so much more and I feel like I'm so very close.

And once the sign for my town passes by my window, and the sense of oblivion enters my bloodstream, a deep voice makes its way into my head —

"Is this seat taken?"

THIS IS FOR YOU

if there's anything you get from this
love
please love
because its worth it
all of it
all the pain and the tears
all the risks and consequences
all the *almost's* and *what if's*
all the beautiful moments you could never forget

love everything
love something
love someone
just love
with every damn fiber of your being
and never stop loving

even when your heart stops
and everything you've ever known changes

just love
on and on

SOMETIMES YOU GET SO ANGRY

"I feel guilty for hating my dad, I try to love him but honestly I can't. And yet, for some reason, I still love my mom even though she cheated. I hate flower, I don't know why but the annoy me. Chocolate sucks. Speeding in cars make me feel alive. I love movies more than people. Music makes me feel when I don't want too. I make promises I can't keep. I've always hated school. I wasn't potty trained until I was five. Orange is the most annoying color. The future scares the shit out of me. I hate how the world is only driven on money. People make me happy and mad. And maybe I am angry all the time and I don't really know how to stop but I am completely and insanely in love with you."

- steven

i dare you to doubt my knowledge

I'M YOUNG BUT I HAVE LIVED THOUSANDS AND
THOUSANDS OF LIVES ALREADY. I THINK I
PICKED UP ON A FEW THINGS.

I MISS WHAT WE HAD

I can love you in the most innocent of ways
Sure, there's sex and hand holding and always finding a
way to brush my arm with yours
who doesn't love that?

but I can show you my love without that

I can look at you and lose my breath every time you smile
my way
I can send you funny and cute pictures of your dream dog
I can leave you funny voicemails to remind you of how
humorous I am
I can listen to your favorite song and watch your favorite
movie
I can ask you how your day was and when it was bad
if we should talk about it
I can pull up to your house and we can take a beautiful
drive because we love the sky and it makes us happy
I can laugh at the way you eat and you can laugh at mine
We can scream out our favorite lyrics and speed down the
isolated highway sticking our heads out the window
We can jump into a random pool and skinny dip and not
touch each other at all — just have races on who can swim
the fastest

and we can sleep together
not fuck, no
sleep

and I can listen to your heartbeat and take in your smell and
not think of another time when I was completely happy

NOW YOU KNOW

my room will always be messy
on my really bad days I don't leave my bed
I can be abnormally stubborn
I don't mean most of my apologizes
I make promises I can't keep
movies and books will always mean more to me
when I'm nervous I bite my nails
occasionally I have really bad panic attacks
my anxiety has gotten worse
hoarding water bottles is my speciality
i cry a lot
like so much
I never say what I mean
I hide too much
my temper is the worst thing about me
i hate too much
i love too much
words hurt and I like that they do
i'm not really good at any relationship
if i've ever loved you there's a high chance I still do
i trust too much
i don't trust enough
being a contradiction all the time fucks me up
i forced myself to like black coffee
i'm selfish
everything I do is for a reason
the sky always matches my mood
i secretly wish i was the sun instead of pluto
i will always love him
i will always love them
i will always love

THINGS YOU SHOULD'VE SAID TO ME

"I trust you."

"This reminded me of you."

"You're something I never encountered before."

"Your mind is radiant."

"You're so lame. I love it."

"I wrote this for you."

"For the love of God, never change."

"I hope you know how beautiful you really are."

"People didn't appreciate you that much, did they?"

"You're too special to forget."

"Thank you for being there for me."

"Tell me all about it."

"I will always care for you."

"I think I will always love you. In this life and the next."

PATIENCE

"why are you leaving?"

"...because it hurt. it hurt to see everyone so happy. I should've been happy, and it killed me to wonder why I wasn't. I felt like I was being lied to about something. I felt like everything people told me about life was a lie. I was missing everything and everyone. It's hard to put into words. But I am not who you think I am. I made you believe in someone that doesn't exist, and I'm sorry for that. I need to go and be who I am, or at least find out who that is. I never intended to hurt you, but what I want... what I need is not here. Something was always pulling me away and I just have to see what that is. I'll regret it for the rest of my life if I don't. This doesn't have to be the end for us, just remember that. I will always want you, I will always care — but you have your own life too. Just know that, if you asked me to wait, Lord knows that I would until the end of time."

UNTIL WE MEET AGAIN

I could start off with some cliche line like —
thanks for all the amazing/shitty times its been real
but I think I'll pass

a lot has happened in my seventeen years of life. Honestly, I was in a pretty bad place for most of it but I think the *ends justify the means.* I failed and accomplished a lot. I fell out of love and tripped heads over heels down a cliff into love. I said a lot of things I should've said long ago, and said a lot of things I shouldn't have in the first place. I have regrets (like most) but I'm happy I do. That means I took risks, and I think that's why I feel so alive now.

there are a lot of people that I won't ever see again. and I'm kind of happy about that. but there are some people that have their names branded on my heart and I will never forget them. I hope I keep in touch with those people and go on regular coffee dates and see them grow into the beautiful humans I know they will become. I hope they don't forget me.

but until then, thank you. even the people that hurt me and the people that changed me (for the better or for worse) — just everyone. thank you for being in my life. I met all of you for a reason and whatever that reason is brought me here. so I thank you endlessly for your lessons and love and hate and everything in between.

I hope we find each other again somewhere.
and I hope it's somewhere beautiful.

PRETENSE

pretend this whole thing was a poem for you
pretend that I became a planet because
you wouldn't love me as a human

ACKNOWLEDGEMENTS

This is one of my favorite things I have ever written. I put my heart and soul into this book and I hope all of you can, not only understand it, but feel it. Thank you everyone who has supported me. Thank you to my loving family, loyal followers, avid readers, and poetry buffs. You have given me so much hope for this book and the rest of my writings. I am forever indebted to your loyalty and love. And to the people who think these poems are about you…

You're probably right.

                                      until next time,

                                            pluto x

ABOUT THE AUTHOR

Ileena *'Pluto'* Irving is a 17 year old girl living in a small town in New Jersey. She has been writing since she was in 4th grade and started to self-publish once she turned 15. She published a story on Wattpad that reached 2 million reads, and she also has a very successful poetic twitter account that has a substantial amount of followers. She has written a poetry book titled *To You, Him, and Everyone Else* and a novella titled *The Art of Being Here.* This is her second attempt at a poetry book and she hopes it has met the expectations of her supporters. She wants to give an extra thanks to her favorite artist on tumblr <u>M1SAKA</u> for the beautiful cover.

CPSIA information can be obtained
at www.ICGtesting.com
Printed in the USA
BVHW08*1131090718
521161BV00009B/136/P